Florence Nightingale

Kay Barnham

WAYLAND

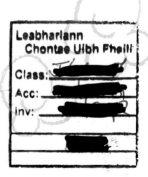

Explore the world with **Popcorn** – your complete first non-fiction library.

Look out for more titles in the **Popcorn** range. All books have the same format of simple text and striking images. Text is carefully matched to the pictures to help readers to identify and understand key vocabulary. www.waylandbooks.co.uk/popcorn

First published in 2009 by Wayland

This paperback edition published in 2010 by Wayland

Copyright © Wayland 2009

Wayland
Hachette Children's Books
338 Euston Road
London NW1 3BH

Wayland Australia
Level 17/207 Kent Street
Sydney NSW 2000

Editor: Katie Powell
Designer: Phipps Design

British Library Cataloguing in Publication Data
    Barnham, Kay
    Florence Nightingale. - (Popcorn. History corner)
    1. Nightingale, Florence, 1820-1910 - Juvenile literature
    2. Nurses - England - Biography - Juvenile literature
    3. Crimean War, 1853-1856 - Medical care - Great Britain
      - Juvenile literature
    I. Title
    610.7'3'092

ISBN: 978 0 7502 6419 8

Printed and bound in China

Wayland is a division of Hachette Children's Books,
an Hachette UK company.
www.hachette.co.uk

Photographs:
Bettmann/Corbis: 5, English School/Bridgeman Art Library/Getty Images: 6, 10, Geoff A. Howard/Alamy: 14, Hulton Archive/Getty Images: 2, 8, 18, Mary Evans Picture Library: 7, The Print Collector/Alamy: 9, 17, Science Museum Pictorial: 11, Alex Segre/Alamy: 19, Adreanna Seymore/Getty Images: 21, William Simpson (after)/Bridgeman Art Library/Getty: 15, Stapleton Collection/Corbis: Cover, 13, Topham Picturepoint/TopFoto.co.uk: 4, WLL/Wellcome Library, London: Titlepage, 12, 16, 20

Contents

Young Florence

Florence Nightingale was born in 1820. At this time, many people were poor and lived in terrible conditions. But Florence was lucky because her family was rich.

Florence, left, and her sister were given a good education.

Rich Victorian women did not work.
Instead, they married, had children
and ran a household. This is what Florence
and her sister were expected to do.

Queen Victoria ruled Great Britain
and Ireland from 1837 to 1901.

People who lived
during Queen
Victoria's rule
were known as
the Victorians.

Florence's dream

Florence believed that God wanted her to help people. She did not want to marry and stay at home.

Florence knew that if she married, she would not be allowed to get a job.

Florence wanted to become a nurse. But hospitals were dirty places. Most nurses were not properly trained.

In hospitals, diseases spread quickly and many patients died.

Nurse Nightingale

Florence trained to be a nurse and cared for poor and sick people. She loved her work, but she wanted to do more.

This photograph of Florence was taken in 1845.

In 1854, the British Army was fighting a war in the Crimea. The Army hospitals in Turkey, across the sea from the Crimea, needed nurses like Florence to help.

The Crimean War was fought between Britain and the Russian Empire.

Can you find the Crimea? It is on the edge of the Black Sea.

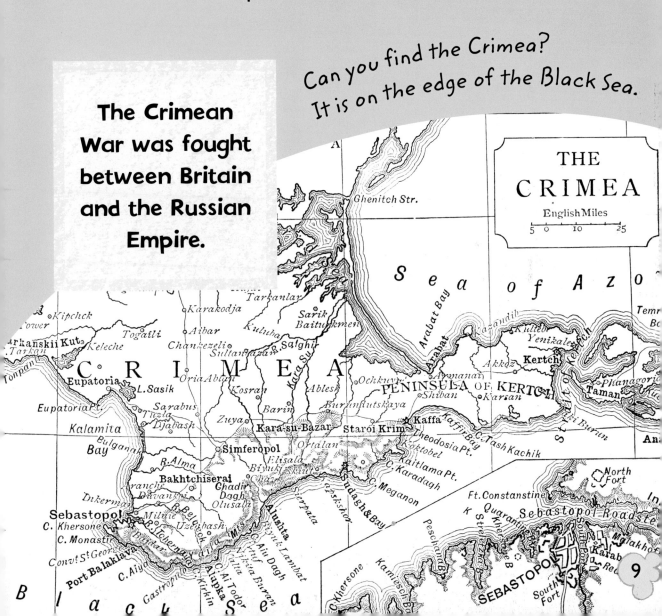

THE CRIMEA
English Miles

9

The Crimean War

Florence went to Turkey with 38 nurses. When they arrived in Scutari, they were shocked at what they saw.

Thousands of soldiers were killed and injured on the battlefields.

At Scutari hospital the filthy wards
were crowded with sick and dying
men. The doctors did not want
Florence to help.

Rats, cockroaches and lice spread disease
throughout the hospital.

The lady of the lamp

More and more patients arrived. Soon the doctors saw that they could not do everything. Florence and her nurses were allowed to help.

Florence, left, made sure the patients were well fed.

The nurses cared for the patients and cleaned the hospital. By night, Florence would visit the wards carrying a lamp, to care for the sick.

Florence became known as the lady of the lamp.

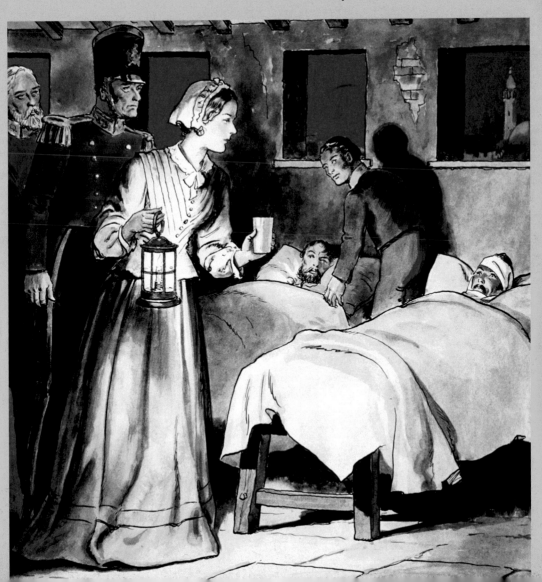

Death and disease

Although Florence made the hospital cleaner, men were still dying. More soldiers died in hospital than on the battlefield.

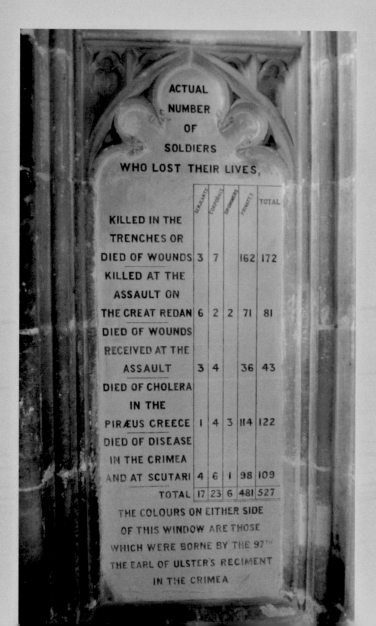

ACTUAL NUMBER OF SOLDIERS WHO LOST THEIR LIVES,	SERJEANTS	CORPORALS	DRUMMERS	PRIVATES	TOTAL
KILLED IN THE TRENCHES OR DIED OF WOUNDS	3	7		162	172
KILLED AT THE ASSAULT ON THE CREAT REDAN	6	2	2	71	81
DIED OF WOUNDS RECEIVED AT THE ASSAULT	3	4		36	43
DIED OF CHOLERA IN THE PIRÆUS CREECE	1	4	3	114	122
DIED OF DISEASE IN THE CRIMEA AND AT SCUTARI	4	6	1	98	109
TOTAL	17	23	6	481	527

THE COLOURS ON EITHER SIDE OF THIS WINDOW ARE THOSE WHICH WERE BORNE BY THE 97TH THE EARL OF ULSTER'S REGIMENT IN THE CRIMEA

This memorial, in Winchester Cathedral, shows how many men died during the Crimean war.

It was discovered that the hospital
in Scutari was built on top of dirty,
old sewers. The water was infected.
Florence was horrified at the news.

When the sewers were cleaned, fewer men died.

Fame!

When Florence Nightingale returned home after the war, she was famous. There were stories about her in newspapers.

Queen Victoria asked Florence to help improve army hospitals. Florence looked at the number of deaths in hospitals and blamed dirty conditions, poor food and disease.

Queen Victoria visited hospitals and saw the changes Florence made.

Nightingale Nurses

In 1860, Florence started a school for nurses. Her students went to lessons and trained on wards, too.

Florence met every one of the trainee nurses.

Florence thought wards should be clean and bright. There should be different wards for patients with deadly diseases.

St Thomas's Hospital was rebuilt in 1868. The architects used many of Florence Nightingale's ideas.

An award for Florence

In 1907, King Edward VII gave Florence Nightingale the Order of Merit. It was the first time a woman had received the award.

Florence wrote books about nursing in her old age.

Florence died in 1910. Every year, nurses around the world celebrate International Nurses Day on 12th May. This was Florence's birthday.

Thanks to Florence Nightingale, nursing is now a career to be proud of.

How to make a sling

You will need:
• A piece of cloth measuring 1 metre x 1 metre

When an arm or wrist is injured, it is often put into a sling. This is just one of the many things a nurse learns to do. Why not practise on a friend? But be sure **never** to move a friend who is really injured.

1. Fold the square diagonally to make a triangle.

2. Lay the cloth under the injured arm and over the other shoulder.

3. Bring the bottom corner up so that it lays over the injured arm.

4. Raise the arm gently and tie the two ends behind the neck.

5. Finally, tuck the spare corner in.

First-aid tips

- Before treating cuts and scrapes, wash your own hands so you don't get any dirt in the cut.

- Ask an adult to help you clean the cut under running water.

- Apply pressure to the cut to stop any bleeding.

- Put a clean plaster or dressing on the cut.

- If you think someone has broken a bone, do not move the injured person. Go and find a grown-up and ask for help.

- If you get burnt by touching a hot object or liquid, run the area under the tap with cool water for 3–5 minutes. Tell a grown-up about the burn.

- If someone has hurt themselves badly, do not move them. Ask for help or phone for an ambulance. **Dial 999.**

Glossary

architect
someone who designs and draws plans for buildings

Crimea
a piece of land next to the black sea. Across the sea was Turkey, where the British army had their hospitals

disease
an illness

infected
when the body is invaded by a germ or virus

memorial
a structure or statue that is built in memory of a person or event

Order of Merit
an award, granted by the Queen of England, to someone who has given excellent service in the armed forces

patient
someone who is ill or injured and who is being cared for

sewers
underground pipes or tunnels that carry away waste water and sewage

train
to learn how to do a job

ward
a large room in a hospital where patients stay while they are being treated

Index